POOLS OF LIVING WATER: DEVOTIONAL POEMS

WRITTEN BY

CAROLYN DAVISON

Copyright © Carolyn Davison 2009

The right of Carolyn Davison to be identified as the author of this work has been asserted by her in accordance with the Copyright, Designs and Patents Act, 1988

All rights reserved. This book is sold subject to the condition that it shall not, by way of trade or otherwise, be lent, re-sold, hired out or otherwise circulated in any form of binding or cover other than that in which it is published. No part of this book may be reproduced, whether by photocopy or by other means nor must any of the content be displayed on a website without prior permission from the author.

ISBN: 978-0-9561573-1-7

To the glory honour and praise of the Lamb who laid down His life for me. My Redeemer, Saviour and Friend who ever pleads for me in glory and who is seated at the right hand of the Father making intercession for His people continually. Praise to His Name which is above all other names.

A PRAYER FOR FORGIVENESS

This poem was written on 6th December 1990, 4 days before I became a Christian

O, Lord Jesus, help me pray
As I attend this glorious day
Open mine eyes so as I can see;
And carry the cross of Calvary

Help me to love and be kind to all
Support me Lord, when I fall.
Guide me through temptation of sin
Into Your Kingdom may I enter in?

Open mine ears so as I may hear,
And serve You Lord through many a year.
Guide me through the valley of death
And all my sins may I confess?

Help me to be a child of Thine
Sinless, loving and divine
And when temptation's at my door,
Help me resist for ever more

O Lord Jesus You died for me,
On that cross at Calvary.
Your suffering saved all my sins
Help me Lord to enter in

Cleanse my soul, so as I may be
By Your side throughout eternity.
As You died to save my soul,
Baptise me Lord, and make me whole

O glorious Lord and Saviour divine
Forgive my sins and make me Thine
With all Your compassion and Your grace
May heaven be my resting place?

A Poem Based on Psalm 1:1-4

Let us be blessed as men
Who love the law of God
Who praise and glorify His name
And rest upon His Word

Let us be like the tree
Which drinks the waters deep
And meditate upon God's word
And all His statutes keep

Let us produce the fruit
Which yields much heavenly good
'Tis manna to the hungry soul
Divine and filling food

WHEN THE LORD SPEAKS

I wanted to have a career
I didn't want to be at home
I wanted to be like other women
So all I did was moan

I wanted to have a big house
I wanted my own car
I wanted lots of holidays
To countries, near and far

But the Lord in all His tenderness
One day, took me aside
And said - "My dear daughter!
These I can provide

"But I didn't call you to go out to work
To have your own career
I wanted you at home so that
You'd have time to draw near

"My Son is preparing a place for you;
A mansion in the sky
You do not need these worldly things
You're the apple of my eye

"So come dear daughter, the one I saved,
Your life is fulfilled in Me.
I will love and provide for you
Throughout eternity!"

So now I see God's plan for me
Is to serve Him in my home
I have a peace all over me
And now I never moan

King of Glory, Prince of Peace

From the glories of heaven
Christ came to sinful earth
Our redeeming Lord and Saviour
Had His human birth.
No kingly throne to sit upon
No crown upon his head
Only a stable, mean and bare
With a manger for His bed

From the place of eternal peace
To a world of strife and war
Our belovèd Lord and Saviour
Came to be the Door:
So sinful man
Could have a throne
And be a diadem in God's hands;
Set up as kings and princes
In a myriad of lands

From the adoring angels
To a world of mocking men
Our blessèd Lord and Saviour
Will one day come again
A trumpet blast to declare Him
Royal robe upon His back
Sinful ones who mock and tease
Will fall upon their bended knees
And see their hearts so black

From a world of sin and death
To a place of eternal life
Christ will take his people
And end all war and strife.
A robe of righteousness He gives,
Upon their heads a crown;
A place of everlasting joy
Without a tear or frown

AT THE FOOT OF THE CROSS

I stood at the foot of the cruel cross
And gazed at Your blood ridden face
I stood there in awe and in wonder
At God's pure compassion and grace
I knelt down and cried out for mercy
My sins nailed You to that cruel tree
You clothed me in God's holy glory
When You died there at Calvary

I stood and I looked up to heaven
And saw Your once piercèd side
I stood there in awe and in wonder
For me Great Jehovah had died!
You looked down and touched me with mercy
Your love and Your grace set me free
And one day I'll stand there in glory
Because You died there, at Calvary.

NOTHING BUT CHRIST IS WORTHY

The Lord must reign within my heart;
With Him, what can compare?
Possessing naught is blessedness
When the Lord God reigneth there

The sins which I possess within
I sacrifice to God
For naught is worthy of my praise
But Jesus Christ, my Lord

I raise my Ebenezer, Lord
Within my sinful heart
For naught will take away Your love
And You will ne'er depart!

WONDROUS GRACE AND LOVE DIVINE

Wondrous Grace and Love Divine;
Jesus, Saviour, Thou art mine!
To the pastures Thou wilt lead.
From Thine Word my Spirit feeds

Glorious Mercy, Tender Heart;
Let me see Thee as Thou art
Loving from eternity
Sacrificing self for me!

Jesus, Saviour, Thou art mine
Wondrous Grace and Love Divine;
Seated on Your throne above
Looking on Your child, in love.

Not that I deserve Thy grace,
But I look upon Thy face!
Tender Mercy, Love Divine;
I am Yours and Thou art mine.

WORDS CANNOT EXPRESS

Words cannot express
How much You mean to me;
The love you showed to sinners
As You died at Calvary.

You came from glorious splendour,
You left Your Father's side;
To choose a beautiful, spotless,
Lovely, heavenly Bride.

You bore such scorn and mocking,
As You hung upon the tree.
You gave Your life so precious,
For sinners such as me

Man would not see the beauty
Of Your divine, eternal face
But on the cross of Calvary
They saw Your love and grace.

You fought our terrible enemy
As You lay in the grave.
Your love had just one purpose,
A people You must save.

Oh powerful resurrection!
Death where is thy sting?
Our Captain of Salvation
Rules over everything.

Now You sit in glory,
At Your Father's right hand;
Interceding for Your people
'Til we join You in Your land.

ETERNAL LOVE

As I gaze at Your face
See wonders untold,
As I gaze at Your hands
Your love just unfolds

As I stand in awe and wonder,
I think of Your love for me;
Your love vast as the ocean
As you died at Calvary

I see Your blood so precious
Run down your piercèd brow.
I see You in the heavens
Interceding for me now.

Oh what love that bought me
With price beyond compare,
One day I'll be in glory
And gaze at Your face there.

Oh help me not to linger
Or tarry in this land
Draw me ever quickly
To Great Immanuel's hand.

SET FREE FROM SIN

Each time I sin
It's as if a chain
Has clasped itself on me;
But Jesus came
To loose those chains
And set the captive free.

Each time I sin
I'm like a bird
Caged, and cannot fly;
But Jesus came
To set me free
So I can soar on high.

Because I sin
The wrath of God
Would be kindled upon me;
But Jesus came
To take that wrath
When He died at Calvary

When I sin
I have to think
Of God's eternal love;
He sent His Son
To take my sin
So I can dwell above.

THE STRAIGHT AND NARROW WAY

Straight was the gate
And narrow the way
When God created
Adam one day.

But Adam decided
To widen the road
He disobeyed God
Took on sin's awful load

So now we see
In this world of woe
The way Adam's heart
Wanted to go

He wanted to rule;
Be a god over all
But because of his pride
Creation did fall

But there is a day
When suffering will cease;
Jesus will come
With His eternal peace!

THERE'S NO ROOM – THERE'S ALWAYS ROOM

THE WORLD:

There's no room at the inn for You;
No peace to sleep and rest!
Go and lie in the creatures' trough,
We're sure that will be best!

There's no room in my heart for You;
It's full of sin and hate!
I'll do what I think is best for me,
God and heaven can wait!

There's no room in the world for You;
We're happy with war and strife!
We'll curse and swear, do what we want,
Because that is our life.

GOD'S RESPONSE:

There's always room at the cross for you;
Dear sinner, the Lord says, "Come!
For I will make you heirs with Christ
And heaven will be your home!"

There's always room in My heart for you;
I sent My Son in love!
He died because you are His joy;
You have a home above.

There's always room in heaven for you;
A place of peace and rest,
A table laid with the finest food,
A home where you'll be blessed

God and Man

Crucify Him! Crucify Him!
A crown of thorns upon His brow.
A purple robe upon His back
Who is this Saviour now?

He is risen! He is risen!
A Crown of glory on His brow
A pure white robe upon His back
In heaven, He's praying now!

Crucify Him! Crucify Him!
Drive the nails into His hands
We hate this man who forgave and healed
We want Him from this land!

He is risen! He is risen!
A sceptre is in His hand
This King of kings saves and heals
He rules over all the lands!

THE NIGHT BEFORE CHRISTMAS – POEM NUMBER 1

'Twas the night before Christmas
And all through the nation
Christians were gathered
With joy and elation;
To celebrate the coming
Of their glorious King,
Who came to clean up
Their hearts full of sin.

He humbled Himself
Came as a babe in a crib
Living on earth
To love and forgive;
Healing the sick,
The lame and the blind
The demon-possessed
And the feeble of mind.

He taught many people
Redemption and grace
To love another
Through the trials they face.
He went to the cross
To show His pure love;
To take on the wrath
Of His Father above

After three days in the tomb
He arose!
Victor o'er death
And the vile hellish foes;
Now He's ascended
To heaven above
The Great Intercessor
With a heart full of love!

So come let's remember
On this Christmas Day
The wonderful Saviour
Who in a crib lay;
Will one day return
No longer a babe
To gather His people
He joyfully saved.

THE NIGHT BEFORE CHRISTMAS – POEM 2

'Twas the night before Christmas
And I think we can bet
That millions of people
Have gone into debt;
To buy special presents,
Some big and some small.
Some will be accepted,
Some not at all

Cupboards are loaded
With excesses of food
Fridges with beer,
Other alcohol too.
Children, excited
Won't go to bed late,
They try to be good -
Make everyone a mate

Nothing will change
As they all grow
'Cause Christmas is about
Goodwill, as you know.
So if someone knocks over
Your drink in the bar
You brush it aside
Just for one day a year

Have you ever stopped and wondered
Why it's not the same
As other celebrations
You could care to name?
Is it really about
A fat man in red coat;
Lights, decorations
And carnival floats?

Is it about getting yourself
Into debt?
Getting uptight
And starting to fret?
Have I bought this
And have I bought that?
I mustn't forget
My dear pet cat!

There's far more to Christmas
Than you could ever expect.
A Man came to pay for
Your life full of debt;
He came to this earth
To live a life we could not
He paid for our sins
When He went to the cross

He was born in a stable,
A manger for a crib
He taught many people
How to love and forgive.
He even loves those
Who mock Him and tease
And try to destroy Him
By the lives that they lead

For 2,000 years people have
Tried to destroy
Every man, every woman,
Every girl, every boy
Who truly believes
That He is the One
Who is their Redeemer
And God's only Son

But for 2,000 years
The church still goes on;
No liberal, no commie
Can destroy God's own Son.
So whether you believe
He came to save YOU!
Have a very Merry Christmas
And Happy New Year too!

TO MY BROTHERS AND SISTERS WHO ARE SUFFERING PERSECUTION FOR YOUR FAITH IN THE LORD JESUS CHRIST

I sit alone in prison
My captors torture me,
Because of who I am
In the One who died at Calvary

They mocked and scorned and beat Him,
Put thorns upon His brow.
They took away His seamless robe,
Stirred up hate within the crowd

They nailed His hands and nailed His feet
To a great big wooden cross;
They jeered and mocked as He hung there;
Not caring about the lost

Alone He hung, left to die.
His Father turned His back
The veil was torn from heaven to earth
The sky became jet black

Looking towards the heavens He cried
Why have You forsaken Me?
Then He gave up His Spirit there
And died at Calvary.

Some people came and took Him down
To place Him in an empty grave
But death could not hold Him long
For He had come to save.

Oh glorious resurrection!
The royal King arose
His victory complete
Against His vile hellish foes.

And now He sits in glory
A sceptre in His hand
And one day all His people
Will dwell in His land.

So as I sit in prison
And gaze upon the Lamb
His love for me
Has set me free;
The perfect, great I AM!

Who is this man called Jesus?

Who is this man called Jesus?
Why did He have to die?
It seems a waste
Of a good man's life!
I want to ask you – Why?

Who is this man called Jesus?
What is His life to me?
He was a good teacher
And healer
Who died at Calvary!

Who is this man called Jesus?
He lived so long ago
How can He
Change my life?
I really want to know!

Who is this man called Jesus?
What made Him best of all?
How can I
Hear Him
Will He ever call?

Who is this man called Jesus?
Why did He come to earth?
What do you mean
I can be born again
I can have a new birth?

I do not understand this man
Who came to deal with sin
You mean I can
Be forgiven
If I will ask Him in?

Why would He want to save me?
Everything I lack
My inward thoughts are
Not the best
And my heart is black as black

You mean He really loves me
Despite what I have done?
He has set His love
Upon me?
God's eternal Son?

You cannot work to get to Him
Just going to church won't do
He wants a personal
Relationship
With just Him and You

So lay aside the things you love
Throw them all away
For the One who died to
Save you
Loves you this very day!

THE VIRTUOUS WOMAN

Who is this wife
So rare and precious
Who has a worth above a gem?
Who is the man
Who safely trusts her?
He is above all other men.

Who is this wife
Who does him good
Who works hard with her hands?
Who cooks with love
She brings him food
From a myriad of lands.

Who is this wife
Rising at night
To feed those in her home?
She works with love
And tenderness
With joy, and not a moan.

Who is this wife?
She sees a field
She buys it for some vines
To grow fresh grapes
So she can make
Some rare and precious wines.

Who is this wife
Who works all day?
Her lamp is lit all night
She spins and weaves;
Makes fine clothes
Her heart just shines with light.

Who is this wife
Who sees the need
Of those so poorly fed?
She reaches out
Her eager hands
To give them living bread.

Who is this wife
Who has no fear
Of snow within her breast?
Her family are
Always clothed
With the finest and the best.

Who is this wife
Of wisdom rare
Kindness upon her tongue?
Glory, praise
And honour are hers
As a song of joy is sung!

Blessed is this wife
Who works
For the glory of her Lord
Strength and virtue
She shall wear
And honour is her word

Deceitful is all
Worldly charm;
Beauty passes away!
But the one who
Serves and obeys the Lord,
A crown will wear one day.

Creation; Crib; Cross; Crown

CREATION:

Before the world was founded,
Before the angels' birth;
The Godhead in all His glory
Made a plan to create the earth

In all their wisdom, majesty
A design began to form;
A word, a breath, a gentle touch:
The universe was born

The day and night, divided
Then sky parted from the land!
Six days all was created
From Christ's eternal hand.

The image of the Creator
Took on the form of man,
The breath of God within him;
The ruler of the land

Then God in all His wisdom
Created a beautiful wife;
From Adam's side he made her
And gave her wondrous life.

They dwelled in a beautiful garden
Communing with their God:
The Lord who had created them
Saw all was very good

But one was angry, full of sin,
Envy, hatred and pride
He came to make the people fall,
He deceived Adam and his bride

A tender fruit hung from the tree
Forbidden by the Lord!
But evil was the one who spoke
Poison from every word.

A bite, a taste, the juice flowed out,
Dripping from their chins;
Their eyes were opened,
No longer innocent
They knew that they had sinned!

God in all His mercy came
To them at cool of day,
But man and woman could not be found
They'd hidden themselves away.

In their nakedness they saw
Their sinfulness and shame.
The Lord in all His tenderness
Called out Adam's name

In fear Adam spoke to the eternal God;
Blame sprung from his heart!
"How could You give me that wife of mine?
She has torn my life apart!"

Eve then pointed to the snake -
It's not my fault, but he
Made me take of the forbidden fruit
Growing on this tree

"Cursed are you!" the Lord did say.
On your belly you shall crawl
I shall send my Son to die for men
Because of this awful fall!

Enmity will go between
You and the woman's Son;
Your head, crushed; His heel bruised,
But salvation will be won

CRIB:

Prophets foretold of a wonderful birth
In King David's town;
He will not wear royal robes
On His head, no crown

A baby born of lowly birth
A manger for His bed.
Cursing, swearing Roman king
Wanting the baby dead.

Incense in the temple rose;
Worship to God the King!
But in the stable lying there
The stench spoke of our sin.

No religious man that day
Understood the Saviour there,
Lying in a creature's trough;
A stable, mean and bare.

But shepherds on the Judean hills
Were greeted with a wondrous sight;
Angels praising and adoring God
Lit up that darkest night

Pagan kings were watching stars
And truly understood,
The Messiah had come to Bethlehem
To do the world great good!

An old man and a widow sat
In the temple night and day,
Waiting for the One who'd come
To wash their sins away!

The Consolation of Israel had come
The Redeemer and blessèd Lord;
But the priests were blind to what was said
In Jehovah's Holy Word.

The heavenly Babe born in a crib,
Came to take away our sins;
He came to quench the wrath of God
To make us heirs and kings.

CROSS:

See the Saviour sitting there
In the place of the Upper Room.
One will go, betray Him
Not a minute or so too soon.

See the Saviour praying there
Sweating great drops of blood;
Praying for those given to Him
With a heart full of love

See the Saviour in the garden:
The soldiers didn't want to miss
The One they'd come to take and kill!
Judas betrayed him, with one kiss

See the Saviour in the court
The One they called the Lamb;
No words sprang forth from His lips
The silent, Great I AM

See the Saviour standing there;
His beard plucked from His face!
I deserved to stand right there
In my belovèd Saviour's place!

They took His robe from His back
His body, the whips did flay!
A crown of thorns was on His brow
That dark and awful day

With all their force they hammered
The nails into His limbs!
He hung there for our redemption:
For all our evil sins.

Mocking, laughing, teasing Him,
A sign above His head,
Pharisees, Sadducees, mankind
Wanting Messiah dead!

The blood of Jesus dropped
Upon the sin cursed ground;
The sky turned black as the darkest night
Creation made a sound!

The veil was rent from heaven to earth;
The Father turned away,
The Son, alone on the cross
Endured what should have been our loss
On that dreadful day.

His redeeming work complete
"It is finished!" He cried out
Bowing His head, He died there!
The Centurion gave a shout

"This man who died, He must be
God's own belovèd Son
He died to take away our sins
He is the only One!"

The Lord in all His glory
Rose upon day three
So that over sin and death
He had the victory.

CROWN:

>See our Redeemer sitting there
>At His Father's right side;
>Interceding continually
>For His belovèd Bride
>
>See the crown of glory
>He wears upon His brow
>The royal robe upon His back
>Where is death's sting now?
>
>See the royal sceptre
>He holds out in His hand
>To all who will accept Him;
>They will dwell in His land
>
>There is a place prepared for us
>A table rich with food;
>A place of peace and sinlessness
>Where all is great and good.
>
>There is a time, we know not when,
>The Saviour, again, will come
>And take His people back with Him,
>Heaven will be their home!

THE SAMARITAN WOMAN

All alone by the well, He sat
With nothing to draw the water,
But soon there came, a woman there;
A shameful Samaritan daughter

"Give me a drink for I have no jar
I cannot reach the water!"
"Why do You speak to me?" she gasped,
"For I am a Samaritan daughter!"

"If you knew the gift of God
I could give you living water.
No longer would you thirst again
You precious, Samaritan daughter!"

"Please kind Sir, I'd love this gift
So I wouldn't need to draw this water.
I would love this gift of eternal life.
Although I'm a Samaritan daughter!"

"Go and fetch your husband here!"
"But I have not one!"
"Five you've had: your words are true!"
Said God's eternal Son

He knew her heart; He knew her life
Had been one of utter shame.
But all are saved who come to Him
And call upon His name

She knew this Man who spoke to her
Was different from the rest
Her life she gave to the Lord
To be full of joy, and blessed

We come to Him just as we are
Nothing can ever be done;
Because the work at Calvary
Was finished by God's own Son

The Dying Daughter

She lay there on her sick bed
Sweat drops on her brow.
Her father was in anguish;
She must be healed right now

Her skin was pale, her body weak,
She found it hard to breathe
Jairus had tried everything
But nothing brought relief

He sat there on His daughter's bed
A tear fell from his eye.
He watched her life slowly slip away.
He prayed to God, "Oh why?"

He ruled the local synagogue
He prayed three times a day
Why did God want to take
His little girl away?

He'd heard about a Teacher
One they said could heal
But could he risk going to Him
How would the Pharisees feel?

They would not want him to go
To the One they call the Christ
But Jairus loved his daughter so
He wanted to give her life

Then he heard a terrific noise
The news was spreading around
Jesus the Great Physician
Was coming to his town

His only hope was to find this Man
Who could fully heal his child
He had heard so much about Him
How He was gentle, loving and mild

Pushing through the excited crowds
He found Jesus and fell at His feet!
He begged and pleaded for Jesus to come
And make his daughter complete

Jesus set off to the house
But people thronged around;
Pushing, shoving from everywhere
No quick way could be found.

Jairus wanted to get home quickly,
His daughter lay near death
For every minute that went by
Could be her final breath

Suddenly the Teacher stopped,
Why does He linger so?
"Who has touched me?" were His words
"Who has touched my robe?"

Jairus wondered why He'd stopped
Time wasn't on his side!
His daughter lay there weak and ill
Perhaps she'd already died

The woman knelt at Jesus' feet,
"Sir, I touched Your hem
Then suddenly I felt your power
I'm fully healed again!"

"My dear daughter, don't you tremble
New life begins right here
Your faith has healed you of this ill
Go, and do not fear!"

Suddenly while Jesus spoke,
A servant came and cried
"You need not bother the Teacher now,
For your belovèd daughter's died!"

The mourners wept, the mourners wailed
They told Jesus He was too late
The little girl had passed away;
That was her awful fate

But Jesus turned to them and said
"She is not dead, but sleeping
Why have you come to this place
With your wailing and your weeping?"

Jesus took Jairus' arm
"Do not fear; only believe,
Your daughter is not dead, you see
Because I can make her live!"

In the house the Master saw
The mother; tears in her eyes,
Jesus took the girl's hand
And said, "Dear child, arise!"

She opened her eyes and sat up,
Her healer she could see.
Jesus turned to Jairus
"A secret, this must be!

"Now fetch your child some food to eat
And give her some refreshing water!
Go, praise God for all He's done.
For giving you back your daughter!"

Jesus is the only One
With power over life and death!
He came, you see
To Calvary
To give us spiritual breath.

JESUS

Bread of Heaven
Manna Divine
Holiest of food
Thou art mine

Rod of Jesse
Spotless Lamb
Perfect, Eternal
Great I AM

Lion of Judah
Prince of Peace
Under your rule
Hate will cease

Perfect, blameless
Sacrifice
Through Your blood
Eternal Life

COME LORD JESUS

Come and touch me with Your Spirit
Come and show Your love to me!
Let me see Your thorn crowned brow
As You hung upon the tree.

Come and fill me with Your Spirit;
Help me empty my heart of pride!
Come and use me as Your servant;
Be my life-long Guide

Come and touch me with Your presence
More of You I long to see!
I want to see You in Your glory
And focus less on me

Come let me see Your beauty
As You intercede for me
Never let me forget
Your work at Calvary

My personal testimony of God's saving grace

MY PERSONAL TESTIMONY

When someone says they are born again – what does it mean? When someone is saved from sin – what does that entail? I am going to share with you my personal testimony of the love of Christ and the grace and mercy of God in my life so far.

Whenever I have thought about my testimony, I have often pondered on the fact that it actually starts long before the world began, in the depths of heaven under the divine counsel of the Godhead. Ephesians 1:4 tells us that we were chosen in Christ before the foundation of the world. It amazes me, even before I was born, God set His love on me in Christ Jesus.

Well, my earthly testimony begins in Cardiff where I was born. My family didn't go to church, but my sister and I were sent to Sunday School. I can't remember much about what was taught there – I only remember a few songs which we learned. By the time I went to high school I'd lost interest in going and only went once a month, when the Guides had a parade service.

I have always been interested in religions and loved to learn about other people's beliefs. I remember telling my sister that if I had to choose a religion I would become a Buddhist, but God had other plans for me.

When I was 17 I was chosen, as a Ranger Guide, to represent Wales in Thailand. What a brilliant opportunity it was to see how other people lived. I was to stay with five different families all over the country. One thing that struck me was the poverty. It was totally different to other countries I had visited, but despite the number of poor people, the temples and idols were covered with gold – copious quantities of it. Many of the idols were still worshipped even though their heads had fallen off – was this really the religion I was interested in? My illusions were shattered.

After coming home I finished off my college course and applied to be a nanny in the UK and also other countries. I went to work in London. By this time my sister had become a Christian and I remember when she told me, I was angry with God as I had been the one interested in religions, not her. Why her? Why not me? Hadn't I been the one reading up on every religion I knew about? Little did I know that God doesn't work like that!

My sister would talk to me about God and the love of Jesus, but I really wasn't interested – I had my work, boyfriend, friends and a social life – why did I want (or need) God?

Across the road from where I lived in Dulwich, London, there was a friend (who I have lost contact with), called Debbie. She was a Christian and asked if I wanted to go to church one Sunday, so I went and got nothing out of it – I didn't go to that church again!

Life drifted on (as it does) and after having a few jobs in the UK, I thought it would be a good idea to go abroad. So I applied for jobs in Germany, Sweden and Belgium – I got the job in Brussels, Belgium. While over there I was encouraged, by my employers, to see as much of the city as I could, but Sundays tended to be pretty quiet days so as I was looking through a magazine I saw an advert for a Baptist church in Wezembeek Oppem. As my sister went to a Baptist church I thought – why not, it will give me something to do! Little did I know that my 'something to do' would lead to a life-changing experience. The first Sunday I went I sat judging everyone, sad person I was! I was sitting next to a mother and daughter from Lebanon and one of them asked me how long I had been a Christian and for the first time in my life I admitted that I had no faith at all! I think admitting that was a break-through although not yet complete.

I went to that church every Sunday from then on and when I got home I started to read my Bible. My sister sent me tapes that her church had recorded – the series was on Hebrews. Amazing ☺

My sister also recommended I read John Bunyan's Pilgrim's Progress – I was hooked. It really got me thinking that there was more to Christianity than just going to church every Sunday and judging people. I devoured it – loving every part! I felt more and more in need of a Saviour – but a Saviour from what? What was I being saved from? Why did I need to be saved? This was new to me - the person who had read about most religions!

As time went on I could see how much I had offended the One who had created me in His image. The life I had led and was still leading was one of rebellion against the One who gave His all for me! In the past I thought all Christians were crazy people, but now I was being drawn to Christ.

On 10th December 1990 after 3 months of searching, by reading my Bible and praying, I gave my life over to the Lord. I saw that only Jesus could bring me back into fellowship with my Heavenly Father. I saw that Christianity is more than a religion – it is a personal, intimate relationship with some**one** – not something! I remember that evening so clearly; I was praying and crying with such agony over the sins I had committed against God, I was asking Him to forgive me and I wanted to turn my life over to Him and turn my life around. At about 9pm it was as if a burden had fallen away from me and a glorious light had entered into my soul – such a relief! For a few weeks before that day I had felt as if I was being pulled in all directions! Now the struggle for salvation was over – but a new struggle was beginning!

Although I have been saved and brought into new life with Christ, I am still not perfect, I am a sinner but one who is saved by grace through faith in the Lord Jesus Christ. I still do wrong things, but there is One who has a heart full of love and forgiveness.

Even though I have been forgiven that doesn't mean I can do what I like because God will forgive me, peace is only given to those who trust and obey. There is no blessing for those who disobey God's commands and do as they please.

Since being saved I have often thought of those who say they don't want to go to church because it is full of hypocrites etc, well, yes churches are full of hypocrites and sinners, but mainly saved hypocrites and sinners! Our focus must always be on Christ – when we take our eyes off Jesus our relationship goes dry and becomes dull and mundane!

Someone said to me a few weeks before I wrote this, that he wasn't good enough to be a Christian because he had led a debauched life, well dear reader, if you are someone who thinks like that, I want to encourage you by saying – Jesus came to save corrupt, debauched sinners! People who think they are too good never come to Christ because they think they can do just as well by themselves! Those who come to recognize they can't 'go it alone' and their lives are so bad they need help are the ones Jesus came to save.

Being a Christian means that you have come into a personal relationship with someone who loves you despite your faults and failings. He cares tenderly for those He saves and promises to protect them and one day will welcome them into His presence in heaven.

Just by going to church doesn't make you a Christian, just by saying a particular prayer also doesn't make you a Christian or doing good works doesn't either. We cannot buy or work our way to God. The only way to come is to bring Him nothing but your sins and failures and to cast them onto Christ.

To sum up in one sentence what being a Christian is – Christianity is all about the Spirit within us.

I cannot boast oh Lord,

Of the work you've done in me

The work was finished, completed

By Christ at Calvary

AMEN & AMEN

www.ingramcontent.com/pod-product-compliance
Lightning Source LLC
Chambersburg PA
CBHW031432040426
42444CB00006B/769